Wicca Candle Spells

*A Beginner's Guide to
Wiccan Candle magick*

Table of Contents

Welcome

Well met, new witches! I'm so glad you're here.

Never before in history have more souls been called to witchcraft. I see it every day: young women searching for meaning in a solemn, gray world devoid of any connection to Mother Moon. Our spirits waste away in a society that denigrates and abuses the divine feminine, attempting to snuff out the light inside of us like the storm does a single, stubborn candle flame. If you're curious about how candle magick can help you better your life and your connection to your own divinity, look no further than this small tome.

I had the luck of being born a hereditary witch, and thanks to my mother's teachings, I've been practicing magick since I was quite small. I grew up in metaphysical shops, where my mother and the whole community of witches taught me how to use candles, crystals, and herbs as tools for spellcraft. I've joined and left covens—even forming my own, read every book on Wicca I could get my hands on, and spent years refining my own variety of ritual magick.

I'm writing this book because I'm called to share what I've discovered along my own path with you, this new generation of witches. Some of us in the older generations believe that a witch's secrets should not be spoken of so easily, but I disagree. The very fact that you are reading this book is all the proof I need to see that you are a compassionate, intuitive soul, worthy of the knowledge of how to use all the tools available to you to manifest your best self.

In these pages, I've used clear, no-nonsense explanations to introduce you to Wicca and candle magick. I've ended the book with a hand-picked selection of candle spells from my own grimoire, but even more than that, I've laid out everything you need to understand *how* candle spells are crafted in the chapters that follow so you can begin to create your own candle spells.

Everything you need is within these pages. All that's stopping you from turning your life into the vision you most desire is yourself.

So! Let's begin, shall we?

Part I: An Initiation into Wiccan Candle magick

Chapter 1: As Above, So Below: The Essential Wicca

I am eager to teach you the secrets of candle magick and share with you spells from my personal grimoire! But before you can cast your first spell as a new witch, you should understand where the magick *comes* from.

Fortunately, many witches have come before you and passed down to us a bounty of spiritual wisdom. Let's begin with a little bit of study for the new witches—and if you're a seasoned witch, you may find this section to be a great refresher course.

So, what exactly *is* Wicca? It's a modern pagan belief system—less organized religion, more intimate spirituality—whose practitioners use ceremonial magick to manifest their will on Earth. These practitioners (regardless of gender) call themselves *witches*.

Wicca was founded in the mid-1900s, but its origins are ancient. Gerald Gardner drew direct inspiration from Western European paganism and folk magick practices when he founded the first Wiccan coven, as well as from hermetic rituals; the result is a powerful blend of pre-Christian deities, ceremonies, and ancient magick from around the world collected into one modern practice.

Since Gardner's time, Wicca has spread and diversified still more. Today, witches are a wildly diverse bunch who perform many varieties of magick, but we are all united in our reverence for the divinity of nature and our powers of magickal manifestation.

The Core Tenets of Wiccan Belief

Witchcraft is deeply personal in nature, so no two witches practice exactly the same way. There are a handful of core principles we recognize as defining Wicca, but in truth, among the various covens and witches who practice today, these tenets are less rules and more strong suggestions.

- **Wiccans worship nature.** Wicca is an Earth-based religion, and while most witches are pagans, *all* Wiccans worship nature. We call the quarters to protect our ceremonial sacred circles and entreat the four elements to lend their powers to our spellwork. Regardless of the deities they may or may not work with, every witch sees the divinity in nature.

- **Witches are connected with the spirit world.** Most Wiccans believe in the spirit realm, and it is commonly accepted that it's possible to commune with the departed. While not all witches are interested in divination and mediumship, the majority believe in an afterlife and recognize that the veil between the Earth and the spirit realm is thin and easily transversed at certain times in the Wiccan calendar.

- **Witches shape reality with magick.** Spellwork is essential to Wicca and is the means by which witches manifest their dreams on Earth. Witches conceptualize magick as a form of energy that can be manipulated through ritual. The source of witchcraft is the life energy in all of us and in everything around us, and thus everyone has the power to perform witchcraft once they understand how it's done.

- **We follow the Wiccan Rede.** The Wiccan Rede is the "golden rule" of witchcraft, which states "An' it harm none, do what ye will". It means that the world is a witch's oyster, and there are no Wiccan laws that govern her magick apart from the commandment to do no harm to others. Not every witch observes the Wiccan Rede, however, and not everyone agrees on what, exactly, constitutes "doing harm." We'll cover only "white magick" in this book, but "gray magick" is out there, too.

- **We observe the Rule of Three.** The Rule of Three states that whatever a witch sends out into the universe with her magick will return to her three-fold; this includes good vibes and prosperity, but negative energies are multiplied as well. Most often, the Rule of Three is cited in regard to the casting of curses and hexes—witches who observe the Rule of Three typically avoid casting harmful spells on the grounds of this "karma." Protection spells are these witches' best friends, as protection magick allows us to defend ourselves from those who would do *us* harm without resorting to hexes; I have several protection candle spells to share with you in Part II!

Manifestation and Intention

So, magick is energy, and witches practice spells and rituals to manipulate that energy, manifesting in reality what exists in our hearts and minds. Modern science has proven that everything that exists vibrates with its own unique energy frequency—including us humans. When a witch learns to recognize, manipulate, and transmute the energies both within herself and without, she can, essentially, bend reality to her will.

Everyone has within them the power to manifest their will—some of us are just naturally more in tune with energies than others. It's a lot like the Law of Attraction, popularized by celebrities in recent years: by putting what you *want* to see out into the universe—your *intentions*—you'll attract what you want back to you. The difference between the Law of Attraction and witchcraft is that witches use rituals and spells to call on powerful energies to aid our manifestations. As you study witchcraft and begin to understand for yourself the innate energy in everything around you, your own powers of manifestation will grow. And the key to mastering manifestation magick? Intention.

Intention is vital when casting a spell; it is through your intention that you specify how energies will be transformed. Your intention should be clear and concise: what is it *precisely* that you want? Writing your intentions down and reciting them out loud offers opportunities to refine and amplify them, but the intention you hold silently in your head and heart is just as important—if not more so.

Blessings and Incantations

The verbal element of spellcasting is traditional in Wicca; it is both a way for us to speak our intentions out into the universe and a means to tap into specific, powerful energies when we cast our spells. You'll see in Part II that many of my own candle spells include spoken incantations and blessings, but not all of them— and it's not absolutely necessary to say them aloud. You can read them quietly to yourself or simply pause and meditate on your intentions when casting.

Perhaps the most common magick words across so many spells and grimoires are "blessed be." This phrase is a way of both cementing our will and giving thanks to the powers that make it possible, and they're typically the last words spoken when closing a spell or ritual.

You'll see "so mote it be" or "so shall it be" used similarly. They all mean the same thing: "My will be done." A longer version of this incantation that I particularly like for closing a spell or ritual goes like this:

As above, so below.
As within, so without.
As the universe, so the soul.
As I will it, so shall it be.

These lines come to modern witches by way of the "Emerald Tablet," an ancient Hermetic text. "As above, so below" speaks directly to the witch's power of manifestation, translating spiritual energy (above) into physical reality (below), as symbolized by the witch's pentagram: a five-pointed star whose top point represents spirit, the four remaining points symbolizing the four elements beneath.

The Four Elements

Wiccan belief and spellwork commonly refer to the four classical elements—sort of the ancient Greek version of today's periodic table. Everything extant in nature can be represented with these four essential concepts; essentially, all matter and energy is divided among them.

Each element is associated with a direction on the compass and has particular qualities attached to it. Witches call upon these elements for their specific powers when casting spells and performing rituals, often using representations of the elements on their altars.

	Earth	Air	Fire	Water
Direction	North	East	South	West
Color	Green	Yellow	Red	Blue
Properties	Nurture, fertility, stability	Intellect, communication, power	Passion, inspiration, action	Emotions, healing, the subconscious

	Earth	Air	Fire	Water
Representations	Herbs, flowers, rocks, crystals, stones, wood, sand, dirt	Incense smoke, feathers, a bell, a fan, a bottle empty of everything but air	Candles, caldron, bonfire	A chalice, vial, or bottle of water, seashells

Wiccan Deities

Wiccans believe in duality and traditionally conceptualize two primary deities, a god and a goddess—the divine masculine and the divine feminine. The divine feminine is often thought of as having three distinct forms: the maiden, mother, and crown, also known as the Triple Goddess, frequently represented by the symbol of two crescent moons flanking a full moon. Within the cycle of the Triple Goddess, as she grows from innocent maiden to nurturing mother and finally to wizened crone, we observe death and rebirth and honor motherhood, both literal and figurative.

However, Wicca is both polytheistic, meaning there are multiple gods and goddesses, and pantheistic, meaning that the entirety of the universe—including all gods and goddesses—are aspects of *one* source of divine energy. Wiccans call upon a variety of deities from many pantheons, including Celtic, Egyptian, and Greek, but ultimately, we believe that these gods and goddesses are all facets of the same divine spirit. Hekate, Freyja, and Brigid are, beneath their trappings, one and the same.

Some witches work quite heavily with a particular deity, others with a wide pantheon, choosing gods and goddesses based on their individual spells and rituals. Here is a small sampling of some of the popular deities from ancient religions:

Name	Patheon	Sex	God of...
Apollo	Greek	M	The sun, music, poetry
Aphrodite (Venus)	Greek	F	Love and beauty
Artemis (Diana)	Greek	F	The moon, the hunt
Athena	Greek	F	War, wisdom

Name	Patheon	Sex	God of...
Bast	Egyptian	F	Cats, sex, magick, secrets
Brigid	Celtic	F	Fire, fertility, craft, home and hearth
Eostre	Germanic	F	Dawn, spring, fertility
Freyja	Norse	F	Love, fertility, death
Frigga	Norse	F	Marriage, prophecy; wife of Odin
Hekate	Greek	F	Witchcraft, the crossroads
Loki	Norse	M	Half-giant trickster god
Lugh	Celtic	M	Warrior-king god of the sun
Odin	Norse	M	War, poetry, wisdom; father of the Gods
Osiris	Egyptian	M	Death, the cycle of life, agriculture
Pan	Greek	M	The wild, nature, nymphs

Name	Patheon	Sex	God of...
Persephone	Greek	F	Spring, death, and rebirth
Poseidon (Neptune)	Greek	M	The sea
The Morrigan	Celtic	F	Triple-goddess of war, fate, death
Thor	Norse	M	Thunder; son of Odin

The Wheel of the Year

The Wheel of the Year is the Wiccan calendar. Witches believe that the changing of the seasons is magickal, harkening back to a time without modern comforts, when the summer harvest was essential for survival through a cold, dark winter. Today, witches pause to honor the changing seasons on holy days called Sabbats and ask for blessings corresponding to each Sabbat's particular energy.

There are eight Sabbats in total: four lesser and four greater. The lesser Sabbats comprise the solar solstices and equinoxes; they are the point of transition between the seasons. The greater Sabbats come to us from pre-Christian fire festivals and are observed at the halfway point between lesser Sabbats when each season is at its height. Witches across disciplines mark these holy days with rites, either practicing solo or celebrating the Sabbat as a group.

Sabbat	Celestial Date	Calendar Date	Festivities and Symbols
Imbolg	Midpoint	February 1	Bonfire, candles, the first stirrings of spring, poppyseed bread, corn husk dolls, hearth and home, the goddess Brigid
Ostara	Spring Equinox	March 21-23	Spring, fertility and abundance, rabbits, eggs, herbs, flowers, the goddess Oestre
Beltane	Midpoint	May 1	Bonfire, May pole, love, fertility, marriage
Litha	Summer Solstice	June 21-23	Bonfire, herbs, flowers, summer fruits, recognizing the coming darkness yet celebrating the height of the sun's

			power
Lammas	Midpoint	August 1	Bonfire, grain harvest, bread, feast
Mabon	Fall Equinox	September 21-23	Harvest, gratitude, thanksgiving, friendship, cornucopia, feast
Samhain	Midpoint	October 31	Bonfire, thinning of the veil, communion with spirits, witches' new year, last harvest
Yule	Winter Solstice	December 21-23	Yule log, wassail, togetherness, recognizing that the sun is coming and the darkest night will pass

The Phases of the Moon

The moon is an essential symbol in pagan magick, representing the divine feminine (while the sun represents her masculine counterpart). The moon symbolizes intuition and the subconscious, calling upon our inner powers—no wonder it is so sacred to witches!

The moon moves through its phases, completing a full cycle about once every 29 days. Each month, we observe the goddess as the Maiden growing into her prime during the waxing moon; she becomes the Mother under the pregnant light of the full moon and finally ages into the wise Crone as the moon wanes. As the lunar cycle progresses, the moon's energy shifts correspondingly. Witches time our spells and rituals, taking advantage of the moon's gifts to amplify our magick.

Phase	Goddess Form	Energies and Symbols
New Moon	None	Intuition, thinning of the veil, communion with spirits, new beginnings, and fresh starts
Waxing Moon	Maiden	Planning and preparation, drawing energy towards you, building towards something
Full Moon	Mother	Manifestation, completion, high energy, creativity, fertility, celebration, emotional upheaval, drawing down the moon
Waning Moon	Crone	Wisdom, reflection, learning, letting go, banishing, protection, self-compassion

A Witch's Tool Kit

Witches use many, many different ingredients and tools as a part of our spellwork; you'll see this at work in Part II. A full list of witch's tools would take up an entire book, so here, we'll look at some of the most essential for a new witch.

- **Altar.** A witch's altar is the sacred space where she practices her craft. Although she certainly may cast spells elsewhere, the altar is like the witch's spiritual home; it is typically decorated with offerings and symbols that hold personal significance to an individual witch. You'll practice most of the candle spells in Part II at an altar, so if you don't have one, get ready by setting one up. You can use any flat surface in your home as an altar, provided it will remain undisturbed.

- **Book of Shadows.** Also called a grimoire, a Book of Shadows is a witch's tome. More than just a spellbook, most grimoires contain lists of magickal correspondences and the witch's intentions in addition to written spells and ritual instructions—think two parts reference book, one part diary. The candle spells I've given you in Part II come from my own personal grimoire, written and perfected over the course of many years.

- **Cauldron.** Nothing calls witchcraft to mind quite like the image of a black cauldron. While you may be most familiar with those large cauldrons from antiquity, heated outdoors over open flames, today, a smaller cast-iron pot on legs makes a fantastic addition to the witch's altar. You can use your cauldron as a fireproof dish for burning herbs, offerings, incense, and candles, but if you don't have a cauldron of your own, any fire-safe dish will do.

- **Athame.** An athame is a witch's ceremonial knife, and they come in many different styles, made of many different materials. An athame is a great tool for directing energy during a spell or ritual. In most traditions, an athame is never used to cut flesh; instead, it's used to cut string/twine and fresh herbs or to carve symbols into candles.

- **Besom.** A besom is a small witch's broom used to energetically clear and cleanse a space such as your altar. It is often made of birch or other natural materials. You can think of the act of using a besom as "sweeping away" negative or otherwise unwanted energies.

- **Bell.** The ringing of a bell marks an energetic shift—often used to mark the beginning and end of a ritual—and symbolizes the element of air on a witch's altar.
- **Wand.** Yes, the classic magick wand. These are commonly made of natural materials; crystal and stone wands are a popular choice, allowing a witch to match the crystal to her particular intentions. Wands, like athames,

are used to direct and transmute energy as a part of spellwork.

- **Chalice.** Water is a common ingredient in spellwork, and witches often use a chalice, goblet, or cup to contain it. Such a goblet can be used to hold an offering or simply to represent the element of water on your altar.

The Sacred Circle

Wiccan ritual magick is commonly practiced within a sacred circle, an energetic space marked off ceremonially to protect witches and their rites from the influence of errant energies. We call this process "casting the circle". This formal element of witchcraft isn't necessary for each and every spell you cast—rather, it's best saved for "special occasions," like Sabbats, and times when you *really* need some extra juice behind your spell.

The candle spells I've given in Part II can all be practiced either with or without casting a circle. While all the intricacies of this practice could fill their own chapter, below are pared-down instructions for casting a circle of your own:

1. Before you start, gather your supplies. You'll need something to represent each of the four elements, such as green, yellow, red, and blue candles—place these at the points of the compass, either on your altar or at the boundaries of your circle—and an athame or a wand to

direct energy, as well as a small bell. You'll also want to include any spell ingredients you'll use once the circle is cast.

2. Determine the boundaries of your circle and how large you need to make it. You can center the circle on your altar or even cast a circle that encompasses your entire home, based on a ritual's specific needs.

3. Walk the circle clockwise three times (if able) and visualize an energetic barrier forming as you do so. "Draw" the boundary of the circle with your athame or wand. If you can't walk the circle, stand in its center, and picture a "bubble" of energy expanding around you to create the sacred space.

4. Next, you'll call the corners. Beginning in the north with earth, light your green candle (or bring your attention to whatever representation you've chosen), then move to the east and light your yellow candle, etc.

5. Once you've completed the circle and lit all four candles, the circle is cast. Say this incantation aloud:

> *From north to east and south to west,*
> *Hail guardian spirits and manifest.*
> *Mother moon, goddess attend,*
> *Within this circle until its end.*
> *To cast this spell, I honor you well.*

My hands steadfast, the circle is cast.

Now, you can practice any spell within your sacred circle, where your energies will remain protected and amplified by these rites.

Note that once the circle is cast, nothing must cross its bounds until the ritual is completed and the circle is "closed." If absolutely necessary, you can energetically "cut" an opening in the circle with your athame and "seal" it closed afterward.

When you're ready to close the sacred circle, visualize the "bubble" shrinking to a point at the center of the altar until it disappears. Ring your bell and say aloud:

And now it's done with harm to none.
As the bell sounds, my spell be bound.
Leave if you must, stay if you will,
Spirits and Goddess, bid me no ill.
Though the circle is open, let it never be broken.
As I will it, so shall it be.

***

And there you have it: your crash course Wiccan primer. With an understanding of the fundamentals of witchcraft under your belt, we'll turn next to the magick of candles in particular. Read on!

Chapter 2: Within the Flame: The Secrets of Candle magick

As you know by now, candle magick is just one variety of magick—though it crosses many, many disciplines. Candles are essential in everything from folk magick to Hoodoo to Gardnerian Wicca. With the basics of witchcraft out of the way, let's take a closer look at candle magick.

The Magick in the Flame

As you learned in Chapter 1, fire is one of the four basic elements. Candles are powerful in magick largely because they so perfectly illustrate and call upon this powerful element—in a size and shape witches can easily handle on our altars! Fire as an element is all about *action*, which makes fire magick a powerful way for witches to see our manifestations at work. But fire can be both consecrating and destructive, and the versatility of candle spells reflects this volatile energy.

Spellwork is about transforming your intention (or a wish, desire, or request) into reality, and candles are one of the best spell ingredients to *communicate* those intentions to the universe. The passion, initiative, and energy of the candle flame burns and sparks, then smokes and wafts, sending your intentions out into the Universe, helping you as a beginner witch clearly visualize the transmutation of energy.

And while candles are most closely associated with the element of fire, they do, in fact, relate to each one of the four elements. Besides the flame of the lit candle for fire, the wick of the candle represents the earth; the smoke and scent wafting through the air represent air; the melting wax signifies the element of water. Thus, the manifestation power in candle magick is amplified with the energies of all four elements.

It's powerful stuff, indeed, but it's easy for a beginner to work with, too! Let's take a look at some of the most essential considerations involved in casting Wicca candle spells.

Varieties of Candles

I'm sure you're aware that candles come in all manner of shapes and sizes, but you might wonder which are best suited for candle magick. The simple answer is all of them! Any candle you use will do the trick, as long as your intention is firm and your spirit open. What's most important is that you practice candle magick safely, using the appropriate container for the type of candle you're burning.

While a candle is a candle, some spells are best served by specific types due to their natures, both practical (like burning time) and magickal (like figurative candles). Let's take a look at the most popular candle types you have to choose from:

- **Tapers.** Taper candles are long, tall, skinny candles, typically burned in candle holders, so named because they taper to a point from a wider base. Taper candles are inexpensive and come in a variety of colors—plus, they have that sort of old-fashioned, *classic* candle look, calling to mind images of ancient magickal rites. Taper candles typically produce larger, brighter flames than other types. They're also easy to dress and carve, making them a particularly popular choice for spellwork—though not as popular as their smaller cousin, chime candles.

- **Chime Candles.** These are the small taper candles you'll find in droves at metaphysical stores, about 4 inches tall and ½ inch around. Candles of this size and shape are quite popular for spellwork for a number of reasons— principally their burning time. It takes about 2 hours for a chime candle to burn all the way down, a great length of time for casting a spell without having to worry about snuffing the candle out and relighting it. Chime candles are inexpensive, easy to dress and carve, and readily available in a variety of colors to match your intention. To amplify your chime candle magick, you can use multiple chime candles at once or repeat a spell with a chime candle over the course of days or even weeks—we'll look at examples of this in Part II.

- **Tealights.** Also called tea candles, tealights are tiny pucks of wax inside a lightweight aluminum casing that serves as a sort of single-use candle holder. They burn quite quickly because of their size, and while you may find them in various colors, white tea lights are much more readily available than any other hue. One benefit of tealights, though, is that they float on water, so they can be a great addition to a spell that involves water magick.

- **Votives.** Votive candles are another popular choice in spellcrafting, easy to find at your local new age shop. They are short and squat, typically no more than 3 inches tall and 1 ½ inches around, and come in a variety of colors— and, unlike the previous types of candles on this list, votives are more likely to be purchased scented. They burn longer than tealights or chime candles but often leave behind a sort of shell of un-melted wax after their insides melt away.

- **Pillars.** Pillar candles are like the votive's larger cousin: tall, broad, and free-standing, these candles vary quite a lot in size. Like tealights, they come in many colors, but the white or colorless ones are most common. Pillar candles take days or even weeks to burn all the way down and almost *always* leave behind a mess of un-melted wax when finished. For this reason, I don't often use pillar candles in spells—however, there *are* some spells (as you'll see in Part II) that require the use of leftover wax after the spell candle is burnt, and pillars are perfect for this use.

- **Container candles.** Any candle that's larger than a tealight and comes in its own container falls into this category. Container candles are made by, well, filling a container with wax, and they vary in size and shape according to the container used—though the most common, by far, is a glass jar. Jar candles are easy to find at virtually any retailer, but they're not often marketed to spellcasters. They usually come pre-scented with essential oils and are almost always white in color. Container candles, in my opinion, are best used as home decor or a bathroom air freshener; I don't use them in my spellwork unless I've made them myself.

- **Seven-day prayer candles.** Seven-day candles or prayer candles are a particular variety of container candle that originated with Spanish-Catholic folk healing not too long ago. As such, you'll find them not only in new age stores but at your local international markets, too, commonly adorned with images of saints. Seven-day candles are excellent because they burn for a long time—about seven days, as the name suggests, if you let them burn continuously—and don't leave behind any used wax. They're also designed specifically for prayer and spellwork, so they come in many colors of wax and are not typically scented. Seven-day candle spells are great for the beginner and for any time you want to hone your spell over the course of a moon cycle or other period. Just be sure to use them safely; you should never leave one to burn unattended.

- **Figurative candles.** You won't find figurative spell candles in many places outside metaphysical shops and internet retailers catering to witches. These candles are designed with spellwork in mind, formed in the mold of a recognizable figure—most commonly human beings, body parts, and witch's symbols like cats and skulls. These are typically more expensive than regular spell candles, but they can add an extra bang to your craft. Candles in the shapes of men and women are excellent for powerful love and romance spells, while candles in the shapes of specific body parts can be used to target meditation and healing.

Of course, you can also make your own candles if you're feeling intrepid. Candle making is a fun craft to pick up, if not a bit messy. I won't go into the specifics of candle making in this book because, as a beginner, I recommend you stick to the simpler stuff. While it's true that you can customize a candle's shape, size, color, and any herbal elements by making your own from the raw materials of wax and wick, as I'll show you in Chapter 3, you can do these same customizations on a regular old taper candle that you've bought at the grocery store.

But what about "special" pre-made spell candles—the ones you buy from fellow witches off Etsy? These are candles that another witch has dressed, blessed, or even made herself from scratch. The creator of the spell candle imbued their magick in it, which, on the surface, sounds like a great idea. A candle with a baked-in spell will be more powerful, right?

Well… not necessarily. See, unless you personally *know* the witch who made the candle, and she made the candle specifically for you and your intention, there is bound to be some misalignment between what *you* want your spell to accomplish and the magick the candle's been imbued with. Oftentimes, these special candles are either far too specific to apply to your situation or so general that your intention won't be properly invoked.

For this reason, I don't recommend these pre-made spell candles. Instead, using the instructions in Chapter 3, you can dress and carve your candle yourself. Not only does this practice ensure that your spellwork aligns with your intentions, but it has the added benefit of strengthening your own understanding of spellcraft and your skills as a witch.

Timing Your Candle Spells

As you learned back in Chapter 1, witches time our spells and rituals to align with natural phenomena, including the phases of the moon and the sabbats on the Wicca calendar, also known as the Wheel of the Year. In Part II, I'll introduce you to some candle spells specific to a Sabbat. You can refer back to the Wheel of the Year section in Chapter 1 for reference at any time.

Remember that each of the four phases of the moon—new, waxing, waning, and full—corresponds with specific magickal energies. By wisely timing our candle spells based on the moon's phases, witches can make the most of lunar magick, "boosting" the power behind our intentions.

- **New moon:** The dark phase of the moon is the best time for spirit work and shadow work—anything that requires one to reach deep within or to reach through the veil that separates us from the spirit realm.

- **Waxing moon:** As the moon begins to grow, we cast spells to draw things into us and start new magickal aspirations, harnessing the increasing lunar energy toward our goals.

- **Full moon:** The full moon is a powerfully magickal time that lends itself well to spells of manifestation as well as cleansing.

- **Waning moon:** As the moon shrinks into a sliver of itself, spells for banishment and release are best timed. We let go of what holds us back as the moon's light wanes.

The days of the week also correspond to specific energies, and we can use these correspondences to time candle spells for greater effect. We can also consider the colors corresponding to days of the week when choosing our spell candles, as well as the ruling planet and zodiac signs of each day, as given in the table below:

Day	Celestial Ruler	Colors	Characteristics
Sunday	The Sun; Leo	Gold, orange, yellow	Healing, vitality, confidence, success, creativity, hope, new beginnings
Monday	The Moon; Cancer	White, silver, pearl, lavender	Intuition, beauty, home and hearth, the divine feminine, emotions, fertility

Day	Celestial Ruler	Colors	Characteristics
Tuesday	Mars; Aries, Scorpio	Red	Action, passion, goal-oriented, destiny, physical activity, sexuality, aggression
Wednesday	Mercury, Chiron; Gemini, Virgo	Light blue, gray, green, orange, yellow	Communication, intellectual pursuits, memory
Thursday	Jupiter; Sagittarius, Pisces	Blue, purple, turquoise	Business, politics, legal matters, good fortune, material goods, money
Friday	Venus; Taurus, Libra	Green, blue, pink, violet	Beauty, love, sex, fertility, friendship, partnership, harmony, art, music
Saturday	Saturn; Capricorn, Aquarius	Black, brown, blue	Protection, duty, discipline, binding, manifestation, completion

Typically, if you're trying to determine the best possible time to cast a particular spell, the moon phase should take precedence over the day of the week—that is, if a spell in Section II suggests that it be cast on a Monday at the full moon, but the next full moon is on a Friday, your intentions would be better served by casting that spell on Friday.

Of course, it may be difficult to time your spell perfectly according to the cycle of the moon or by certain days of the week. Sometimes, a cord cutting simply needs to happen *stat*—when energies are high and you need ritual magick, there's no sense in waiting weeks for the proper moon phase. Timing our spells by moon phases and days of the week helps amplify our magick, but so do any number of other correspondences, such as the herbs and oils with which we dress our candles (which we'll discuss in detail in Chapter 3). So, if the timing isn't perfect, don't sweat it.

Divining Flame and Smoke

When a seer stares into the flames or billowing clouds of a bonfire, looking for a message or a sign, this is called *scrying*. To scry, from the Old English *descry* meaning "to discern," is to gaze intently at an object and interpret any visions one may find within. Scrying can be done with virtually anything that you can "stare into." You're almost certainly familiar with the crystal ball as a tool for divination, but dancing flames and swirling smoke were most likely some of the very first scrying mediums.

Scrying isn't easy, and it doesn't come naturally to all of us. To see images in smoke and flame requires *clairvoyance*, or the ability to discern more than what's in front of you with your vision. I personally prefer to stick with methods of divination that are more structured in their symbolism—but fortunately, you have an opportunity to interpret clear messages in your candle spells, as well.

Interpreting the shapes and movements of the flame and smoke of your candles can help you glean a great deal of insight into the efficacy of your spell and the intensity of energies surrounding your magick, and you don't need psychic powers to do it—just a little intuition and a keen eye. Your spell candles are trying to tell you something, and you can translate that message, provided you have a basic understanding of the symbolism.

Here are the possible interpretations for your spell candle's flame:

If your candle flame is...	This means...
Clean burning, normal	Your message is being heard or your intention is being sent into the universe clearly and effectively
Especially big	This magick is very potent, and you're

If your candle flame is...	*This means...*
or bright	likely to get what you want out of the spell; if what you want doesn't manifest right away, take this as a sign that you're on the right track
Small but steadily burning	Your spell is working, but your magick is weak; perhaps your intentions lack focus— or your *true* intentions are not what you've spoken to the universe...
Small and weak, almost swallowed by wax	The power you want to manifest is out of your reach—you're asking too much, your intentions don't match your spell ingredients, or the timing is wrong
Popping and hissing	May indicate that some other force is working against you, such as a binding spell that is blocking your magick; can also be a sign that spirits are trying to communicate with you
Dancing or flickering	If your candle flame is making a lot of movement, this is an excellent time to try your hand at scrying—see what its particular dance tells you; in general, a

If your candle flame is...	This means...
	flame like this means that very powerful energies are afoot
Blue in color	A blue flame (as opposed to the typical yellow or red-orange color) indicates remarkable potency, either through your own magick or because very powerful spirits are nearby
Extinguished on its own	Do not relight the candle; the spell is complete, either because it's successful or the universe is telling you "No"
Unable to be extinguished despite snuffing	Your spell is *not* complete; let the candle continue to burn, and if possible, repeat the spell again—after reviewing your intentions and ingredients for clarity
Non-existent—your candle won't light at all	Take this as a sign to put down your tools and step back; think about what you're trying to accomplish and what may be blocking you; try cleansing your altar or other sacred space

Now, typically, a well-made candle *shouldn't* produce much smoke until you snuff out the flame, but anointing your candle with oils and dressing it with herbs can change this. Here are interpretations for particular varieties of candle smoke:

If your candle's smoke is...	This means...
Abundant or long-lasting	Take this as an invitation to try scrying— look deeply into the smoke and notice if any visions or words come to you; alternatively, this can signal that the element of air is hard at work bringing your spell to fruition
Drifting away from you	In general, your magick is moving away from you, out into the universe, but any interpretation of the direction smoke travels is dependent on your intentions—if you *intend* to send energy outward, you've succeeded, but if this is an inward-looking spell, you may have some reworking to do
Drifting towards you	In general, power and blessings are coming to you; but if the energy you're sending out is targeted at another person, this may be a sign that you will be caught in the crossfire

If your candle's smoke is...	This means...
	of your spell
Leaving soot in the candle holder or container	If the soot only covers the top of the material, it's a good sign that your magick is working. If the soot blankets the entire container, it's likely that the Universe is telling you "No," but you can also interpret specific shapes in the soot, as one does with tea leaves, to glean a more specific message
White in color	Your intention has been heard, and your spell is likely to be successful
Black in color	Typically, your spell is not going to be successful; take it as a sign to reexamine your intentions and spell ingredients before trying again

Still, as with all magickal elements, you should put your intuition first. If your gut tells you that your flickering flame or swirling smoke means something specific, listen to it—after all, *you* have a better understanding of your own magick and intentions than any book. Over time and with practice, you may come to define your own set of flame, wax, and smoke interpretations for your book of shadows.

Practical Considerations

Finally, there are a few practical matters to consider when it comes to candle magick.

We're casting with fire, here—literally—so you've got to practice safely. This means always using the appropriate candle holder for the type and size of candle you're burning, ensuring that your burning candles are kept away from any flammable materials, and preventing children or pets in your home from disturbing lit candles.

On that note, you may have heard that you're never supposed to put out a spell candle, that you have to let it burn out on its own—but this is only partially true.

It's OK to snuff out a spell candle. In many cases, it's necessary for the safety of you and your loved ones—you should never leave a candle burning unattended unless it's in a perfectly fireproof container, like your fireplace. It's also necessary to put candles out as part of some spells; you'll notice in Part II that I've instructed you to snuff out and relight candles at particular times.

The important thing is that you don't *blow out* your spell candles; doing so is a symbolic act of blowing your intentions away. Instead, use a tool specifically designed to snuff out the flame. These are readily available from online retailers or new-age shops.

You may also want to consider the material from which your candles are made. Paraffin wax is commonly used to make candles, but this is a byproduct of toxic petroleum. If you're environmentally-minded or concerned for the health of those in your home who will breathe in this stuff, avoid paraffin candles and opt for natural waxes, like soy and beeswax.

***

I hope you've found this introduction to the power and practicalities of candle magick quite *illuminating*. (See what I did there?) You're beginning to build a solid foundation for casting candle spells with confidence and intuition.

Next, I'll introduce you to methods for enhancing candle spells with colors, herbs, runes, crystals, oils, and more. This is where the magick *really* happens!

Chapter 3: Candle Correspondences: Colors, Herbs, Runes, and More

Now that you understand the basics of candle magick, including how to choose your candles and time your spells, we'll dig deeper into the secrets of candle magick, looking at correspondences. Correspondences tell us the inherent magickal properties of every material we use in spellwork, from colors to flowers, from totem animals to crystal geodes. These magickal properties come to Wicca from a number of sources, including psychology and various pagan practices.

A complete list of magickal correspondences could fill a book—and indeed, many such encyclopedias can be found out there. In this chapter, we'll focus on some of the most common and useful correspondences specific to candle magick. As a new witch, I believe it's best for you to keep it simple to avoid feeling overwhelmed. There are so many options out there that sometimes, it can feel paralyzing! So, I've chosen the herbs, crystals, symbols, and more I reveal in this chapter very intentionally. Later, in Part II, you'll find spells that utilize the ingredients and symbols listed here, and nothing more. Think of these correspondences as a starter kit and add to them in your book of shadows as you develop your ritual practice.

With that, let's get to it.

Choosing a Candle Color

Color correspondence is used throughout witchcraft and other new age practices, from selecting stones that correspond to particular chakras in the body to the brightly colored ribbons witches wind around the Maypole at Beltane—but perhaps nowhere else is color so significant and so useful as in candle magick.

Witches choose the color(s) of candles in our spells based on our intentions, and in doing so, we raise power for our manifestations. For instance, you'll want to choose a green candle for a spell to draw money in but an orange candle if your spell intends to ignite your creativity. (You'll see what I mean more in-depth in Part II.)

There are two interpretations for the meanings of colors in candle magick. First, the color itself is light—electromagnetic energy, in other words—and each color in the rainbow emanates a specific vibrational frequency. In this way, colors have an innate energetic value in witchcraft. Perhaps more important, though, is the *psychological* interpretation of color. When we see colors, they trigger subconscious responses, calling up images from the depths; archetypes based on what we see in the natural world, which are often shared across cultures.

Color interpretation does vary by culture and change over time—for instance, we in the United States didn't begin to associate pink with girls and blue with boys until the early-mid 19th century. Still, some associations run deep. The list of interpretations I've given below comes primarily from Western European Wicca. In this (as in all things witchy), you should trust your instincts and intuition first and foremost. If a color has a specific meaning to you, then use that correspondence. Your goal is to bolster your spell intentions, not to feel limited by rigid color associations.

- **White.** Purity, protection, safety, spirituality, peace, enlightenment, connection to the higher self, focus, freedom, initiation, the moon

- **Black.** Protection, balance, transformation, manifestation, divination, banishing, binding, personal sacrifice, absorbing negative energy, the new moon

- **Brown.** Family, stability, security, home, generosity, decision making, concentration, grounding, animals, earth

- **Red.** Passion, strength, motivation, ambition, action, courage, sex, desire, power, business deals, confrontation, fire

- **Pink.** Self-love, romance, friendship, partnerships, new beginnings, femininity, nurturing, compassion, healing, harmony, joy

- **Orange.** Ambition, opportunity, mental awareness, success, creativity, strength, dominance, harvest time, relief from depression

- **Yellow.** Intelligence, confidence, memory, logic, productivity, positivity, joy, self-esteem, friendship, air, the sun

- **Green.** Fertility, abundance, money, growth, career, trust, rebirth, new beginnings, growth, luxury, grounding, earth

- **Blue.** Tranquility, healing, patience, learning, meditation, introspection, communication, wisdom, clarity, peace, water

- **Purple.** Wisdom, spirituality, intuition, clairvoyance, authority, healing emotional wounds, communicating with spirits

- **Gold.** Divine masculine energy, spiritual attainment, luck, money, prosperity, the sun

- **Silver (or gray).** Divine feminine energy, psychic powers, divination, secrets, astral travel, seeking hidden truths, the moon

If you don't have a particular color of candle on hand when you need it, don't worry—a white spell candle will always make an acceptable substitute. Color is only one of many ways to align your intentions with your manipulation of energies. While the right colors will amplify your powers, the same can be said about the number of candles in your spell, the moon phase in which it's cast, the oils (if any) you've anointed your spell candles with, and more.

The Influence of Numbers

Like colors, numbers, too, exert innate energies over us and trigger unseen psychological responses. The ancient Babylonians believed that single-digit numbers were the building blocks of the universe, and this idea carried over to the ancient Greeks, who popularized numerological study. Ancient Greek philosopher and mathematician Pythagoras posited that everything in existence could be broken down into representative single-digit numbers, a concept that then passed into Hermeticism and made its way to modern witches.

Numbers are everywhere in witchcraft; they are an essential piece of symbolism in astrology, tarot cards, ritual, and even witch's law, as with the Rule of Three. When it comes to candle spells in particular, numbers serve a few different purposes, including:

- The number of candles used in a spell.
- The number of times an incantation is repeated when lighting a candle.
- The number of times a candle is lit and snuffed out.
- The number of hours or days that a spell candle burns.
- The number of drops of oil or sprigs of herb a spell candle is anointed/dressed with.
- The number of sigils or runes carved into a spell candle.

I'm sure this sounds like a lot to consider, especially if you're not fond of numbers! But don't worry, there's no math involved aside from simple counting, and I'll show you exactly what I mean by each of these examples when we get into the spellbook in Part II.

For now, let's take a quick look at what each single-digit number represents. As with colors, the meanings of numbers can vary based on culture; for example, 4 is considered *very* unlucky in China, and 7 is a holy number to Christians. In writing the interpretations below, I've used primarily Pythagorean or "western" numerology, as well as associations specific to witches.

1. The primordial number, primal energy, beginnings, potential, willpower, the self, all-encompassing

2. Balance, partnership, lovers, duality (god and goddess, light and dark, life and death), opposites, harmony, the ties that bind

3. The witch's number, manifestation, divinity (e.g., maiden, mother, and crone), creativity, joy, celebration, self-expression, karma

4. Foundations, home, the Earth, control, pragmatism, the four corners, the four elements, the four seasons

5. Freedom, adventure, risk, the pentagram, the five senses, marriage, humanity (five fingers), the "fifth element:" you as the spellcaster

6. Healing, service to others, creativity, harmony, joy, beauty, love

7. Spirituality, intellect, truth-seeking, amplification, a cycle (e.g., days of the week), philosophy, the metaphysical

8. Success, ambition, wealth, manifestation, power, control, infinity, the energy of the universe

9. Wisdom, completion, awakening, spiritual knowledge, three times three (so amplifies all the qualities of the three)

As with color correspondences, your own personal interpretations of numbers are important, too. If a number holds particular meaning to you, use it accordingly in your candle magick.

Dressing a Candle with Herbs and Oils

Herbs, flowers, and spices—truly, every part of a plant, from root to seed—have intensely magickal properties, and so-called green magick is a vital part of witchcraft traditions around the world, including Wicca. Witches use plants to brew potions, infuse oils, create talismans, burn as incense, and so much more. From the memory-stirring magick of a rosemary sprig to the invigorating aroma of cinnamon—and everything in between— herbs are a powerful tool in any witch's arsenal.

What's more, herbs and oils make the perfect companions for your spell candles. By dressing a candle in intentionally chosen plant ingredients, we can imbue our candle spells with the magick of the Earth, working powerfully alongside the fire energies of our burning candles. As when choosing a candle color, the herbs and oils you use to dress and anoint your spell candle must align with your intentions in order to amplify and direct your magick.

For simplicity's sake, I've combined all types of plant ingredients in the table below. Some are blossoms, others are roots, still more are trees; some are easily found in your spice cabinet, while others might require a trip to the metaphysical shop. But each ingredient I've chosen, whether you use it in its whole form or as an essential oil, is a fantastic choice for your growing collection of spell ingredients.

Ingredient	Description	magickal Properties
Allspice	Common in spice cabinets, a type of dried berry	Business, luck, success, money
Althea (Marshmallow)	Flowering medicinal plant	Cleansing, goodwill, healing, psychic abilities
Balm of Gilead	Buds of the black cottonwood tree, long used medicinally	Grief, healing, mending, forgiveness
Basil	Leafy herb common in kitchens	Protection, fertility, cleansing
Birch	White-barked tree, may be used in EO form	Concentration, creativity, protection, inner calm
Catnip	Variety of mint, common in gardens	Love, luck, dreams, spirit
Cedar	Fragrant evergreen tree, often used in EO	The afterlife, spirit, clairvoyance, protection

Ingredient	Description	magickal Properties
	form	
Chamomile	Small white flowers with yellow centers	Blessings, male energy, luck, the sun
Cinnamon	Sweet and spicy bark, commonly found ground or as whole sticks; the leaves of the plant can be used also	Wealth, money, security, luck, attraction
Clove	Spicy dried flower buds of the clove tree	Divination, intuition, truth, vision, prosperity
Cumin	Spice made from the seeds of a type of parsley plant	Fidelity, harmony, longevity, the home
Cypress	Fragrant evergreen tree	Binding, protection, comfort, mental power
Dandelion	Flowering weeds common in yards	Clairvoyance, divination,

Ingredient	Description	magickal Properties
		communication, spirit
Dill	Aromatic herb common in gardens	Protection, love, sex, money
Eucalyptus	Aromatic evergreen tree, most commonly used as an EO	Balance, calm, concentration, focus, invigorating
Fennel	Flavorful leaves of a flowering herb	Blessings, protection, luck, abundance
Frankincense	Resin from the Boswellia tree, most commonly used in EO form	Cleansing, purification, meditation, consecration
Garlic	Bulb of the garlic plant, commonly found in kitchens	Justice, protection, banishing, security
Ginger	Root of a flowering plant, commonly found in kitchens	Pregnancy, childbirth, unity, success

Ingredient	Description	magickal Properties
Honeysuckle	Flowering bush with a sweet fragrance	Love, happiness, peace, wellbeing
Jasmine	Highly fragrant vining flower	Love, sex, relaxation, prophecy
Juniper	Berries of the evergreen juniper tree	Fertility, happiness, optimism, spirit, strength
Lavender	Fragrant flowering herb popular in gardens and as an EO	Rebirth, manifestation, tranquility, sleep
Lemon	Fruit of the lemon tree, common in kitchens	Happiness, joy, cleansing
Lemon Balm	Lemony variety of mint	Success, clarity, relationships, business
Lemongrass	Fragrant edible grass	Divination, psychic abilities, improving concentration, love,

Ingredient	Description	magickal Properties
		purification
Lime	Fruit of the lime tree	Energy, purification, love, money
Mandrake	Root of the Mandragora plant	Courage, desire, spirit, binding
Mistletoe	Winter berries of a plant that grows parasitically on trees	Blessings, luck, new beginnings, Yule
Mugwort	Aromatic flowering herb	Psychic powers, intuition, dreams, spirit
Nettle	Herbaceous flowering plant common in yards	Healing, justice, protection, confidence
Nutmeg	Spice made from the seed of the nutmeg tree	Life, luck, love, attraction
Oak	Tall deciduous tree—often the leaves are used in magick	Confidence, justice, luck, wealth, independence, strength

Ingredient	Description	magickal Properties
Orange	Fruit of the orange tree	Love, divination, luck, money
Patchouli	Fragrant flowering plant	Manifestation, attraction, confidence, willpower
Pepper	Spicy dried fruit of a flowering vine	Security, binding, protection, strength
Peppermint	Variety of mint	Dreams, visions, creativity, revitalization, healing
Pine	Fragrant evergreen tree, common as an EO	New beginnings, blessings, hope, prosperity, release
Red Clover	Herbaceous flowering plant	Love, fertility, luck, protection
Rose	Fragrant flower	Fertility, family, blessings, love, happiness
Rosemary	Woody herb common in	Intellect, protection, energy, memory

Ingredient	Description	magickal Properties
	gardens	
Sage	Fragrant flowering herb common in gardens; white sage is the variety most commonly used in ritual magick	Protection, purification, banishing, longevity
Sandalwood	Aromatic yellow wood, most often used as an EO	Focus, concentration, blessings, success
St. John's Wort	Yellow flowering herb	Divination, purification, dreams, happiness
Star Anise	Spicy star-shaped seed pod from a variety of evergreen tree	Blessing, spirit, love, immortality
Sunflower	Bright yellow flowers that grow in summer	Clarity, luck, money, the Sun

Ingredient	Description	magickal Properties
Thyme	Leafy herb common in kitchens	Healing, happiness, abundance, rebirth, calm
Violet	Sweet little purple flowers	Innocence, faithfulness, modesty, humility
Wormwood	Leafy medicinal plant, favored by witches and makers of absinthe	Clairvoyance, dreams, spiritual guidance, the Moon
Yarrow	Flowering medicinal plant	Protection, banishing, marriage, healing, release
Ylang Ylang	Flower of a tropical tree	Love, sex, calm, emotions

Anointing a candle in oil is quite easy, especially if you're using a regular chime candle or taper candle. Simply hold the candle upright in one hand and use your essential oil dropper to apply the oil. For most spells, you'll start at the tip of the candle (but avoid the wick itself) and rub the oil downward to anoint, but for other spells, you'll start at the bottom and work your way up. The difference is in your intention and how you're working with the energies present; witches draw the oil downward to bring our intentions into reality and push it up and away to release unwanted energies.

You can use oil alone or, once your candle is anointed, you can add dried flowers, herbs, and spices. The oil should help the plant matter stick to your chime or taper candle. Simply sprinkle it on top or roll the candle gently in your ingredient(s). This is what we call dressing a spell candle, and you'll see this in action in the spells in Part II.

Carving a Spell Candle

A spell candle makes the perfect canvas for literally writing out your intentions or drawing symbols that represent them. It's pretty simple: just use your athame (or any *spiritually cleansed* tool with an edge or point) to etch your message into the wax. I find it's best to do this as part of my spellcasting (within the sacred circle, if I've cast one), rather than beforehand; this way, I'm in the moment, in my element, and focused on my intention when I carve my candle.

If your intention is too long and complex to be carved into a chime candle (or whatever size candle you're using), you have a few options. One, you can write your intention on a piece of paper instead—you'll see how I've instructed you to do this in some spells in Part II. Two, you can try condensing your intention down to a single word or short phrase, and as long as you have its full meaning clear in your heart and mind, this will do fine. Finally, you can use a symbol to represent your intention. Two popular choices for symbols are sigils and runes.

A *sigil* is a symbol you create yourself. When you pen a sigil, you put not only your intention but all the energy and power *behind* your intention into that sigil, making it a very powerful symbol. A sigil doesn't have any inherent meaning based on its shape; its meaning is all about the process of its creation. This is why it's essential to make your own sigils, not to use those you may find online. What the sigil actually does is bypass your senses and conscious mind, channeling energy and intention straight from your soul to the page.

There are many, many ways to create a unique sigil—but since this is a candle spellbook, here's just *one* short and sweet method to turn your intention into a sacred symbol.

1. Write out your intention, e.g. "Everything I need is at my fingertips."

2. Remove duplicate letters, e.g. "E V R Y T H I N G D S A M F P"

3. If you have too many letters to work with after removing duplicates, try removing vowels, as well, e.g. "V R T H N G D S M F P"

4. Then, you simply combine these letters into an image. There are no right or wrong ways to do this, provided you are meditating on your intention all the while. Try drawing the letters over top of one another and connecting them. You can erase some lines, add new ones, embellish, flourish—whatever feels right to you.

5. And here's the key: once you've carved your sigil into your candle, you need to *forget it*. Don't focus on your sigil, don't memorize what it looks like, and don't use it for a second spell.

Here's an example sigil I created for "Everything I need is at my fingertips." If you squint, you can make out every consonant—but again, once you've put your energy into your sigil, you don't want to spend much time looking at it or, Goddess forbid, over-intellectualizing it.

Another popular choice for carving candles is *runes*—Futhark runes, to be exact. These are letters of the ancient Nordic alphabet, and each rune is not only a letter but has a specific spiritual meaning tied to it. Runes are commonly used by witches and other new-age practitioners for purposes of divination; a set of runes carved into small bits of wood, bone, or stone are kept in a bag, and the witch draws one or more at random and interprets their meaning.

But Futhark runes can also be worn as talismans, etched on walls, and carved into candles to amplify your intentions. Take a look at the table below to find the rune or runes associated with your spell's aim.

Symbol	Name	Literal Meaning	Interpretation
ᚹ	Fehu	Cattle	Wealth, abundance, luck, a windfall
ᚾ	Uruz	Ox or bull	Strength, endurance, power, accomplishment, masculinity
þ	Thurisaz	Giant or thorn	Thor's hammer; aggression, power, danger, impulse, anger
ᚠ	Ansuz	God or mouth of a	A message; strongly associated with Odin, the

Symbol	Name	Literal Meaning	Interpretation
		river	father of the Norse gods; communication, truth, language, good advice
R	Raidho	Road	A journey; a wheel or cycle; travel, progress, spiritual growth
ᚲ	Kenaz	Torch or flame	Illumination of knowledge, creativity, inspiration, secrets revealed
ᚷ	Gebo	Gift	Blessings, generosity, an exchange, talents
ᚹ	Wunjo	Joy	Peace, reward, friendship, togetherness, pleasure
ᚺ	Hagalaz	Hail	A great trial, a test of will, a cataclysmic event, destruction, challenge
ᚾ	Nauthiz	Distress	Human need, necessity, desire

Symbol	Name	Literal Meaning	Interpretation
I	Isa	Ice	Illusion, ego, beauty, risks
ᛃ	Jera	Year or harvest	Balance, the passing of time, slow and steady progress, abundance
ᛇ	Eihwaz	Yew tree	Inner transformation, death, endurance, protection
ᛈ	Perthro	Destiny	Luck, karma, fate, rolling with the punches
ᛉ	Algiz	Elk	Protection, guidance, divine connection
ᛋ	Sowilo	The sun	Celebration, willpower, true purpose, guiding light
ᛏ	Tiwaz	Arrowhead	Represents the god Tyr; victory, judgment, leadership, truth
ᛒ	Berkano	Birth tree	New beginnings, the divine feminine, the cycle of birth and death

Symbol	Name	Literal Meaning	Interpretation
ᛗ	Ehwaz	Horse or steed	Harmony, partnership, speed, forward motion
ᛘ	Mannaz	Man (humankind)	The self, cooperation, the greater good
ᛚ	Laguz	Lake or sea	Emotion, intuition, mystery, creativity
ᛜ	Ingwaz	Hero or seed	Connected with Ing, a hero of Norse myth; fertility, creation, potential, wellbeing
ᛟ	Othala	Estate or inheritance	Legacy, ancestors, wealth, history
ᛞ	Dagaz	Dawn or daybreak	A breakthrough, a gateway, change, enlightenment

Crystal Companions

Crystals, gems, and stones are popular spell ingredients because they have incredible innate powers—and they're beautiful, to boot. Crystals come from the Earth (or, sometimes, from other planets and satellites) and most are millions of years old. What makes a crystal a crystal, is its highly ordered chemical structure, called a crystal lattice. A crystal lattice is like a fractal, repeating the same geometric pattern of vibrating molecules. As such, crystals contain a *lot* of energy. At first glance, you may think crystals and stones don't work quite as well with candle magick as do herbs and oils, but it isn't difficult to work stones into your candle spells.

Some of the premade spell candles you can buy already imbued with magick contain small stones or chips of crystals. If you're up for making your own candles, you can certainly try this, but I'll tell you from experience that it's more effort than it's worth—unless you pour your candle wax in multiple layers and let it dry between each, your crystals will all sink to the bottom of your jar!

One great way to combine crystals with candles in your spells is to burn a candle on top of or next to a stone. Once the candle has melted away, you can carry the stone with you or sleep with it under your pillow to keep the magick of the spell near to you long after the flame is extinguished. We'll look at this and more examples in Part II.

There are thousands of varieties of minerals out there and at least a hundred that are loved by witches for their magickal properties. Here's a much-abbreviated list of stones I'd personally consider essentials for the new witch.

Stone	Color	magickal Properties
Amber	Yellow-orange	Healing, rejuvenation, empowerment, joy, happiness, warmth
Amethyst	Purple	Psychic powers, divination, sleep, dreams, intuition, breaking addictions
Aquamarine	Light blue	Tolerance, lack of judgment, inner peace, intellect, communication, healthy pregnancy
Carnelian	Red-orange	Passion, sex, success, drive, ambition, confidence, creativity, overcoming negativity or abuse
Citrine	Yellow	Energy, balance, joy, delight, wealth, prosperity, self-

Stone	Color	magickal Properties
		esteem, intellect, creativity, concentration
Clear Quartz	White/clear	Very high vibrational energy—an all-around spiritual cleanser and amplifier
Garnet	Dark red	Invigoration, regeneration, fire, love, passion, perception, energy, power
Hematite	Black/gray	"The stone of the mind," intellect, memory, protection, grounding, focus, strength
Lapis Lazuli	Deep blue	Communication, awareness, clarity, stress relief, cleansing, soothing, spiritual guidance
Malachite	Green	The heart (both physical and spiritual), healing, dreams, protection, growth, change
Moonstone	White/cream	Moon magick, the Goddess,

Stone	Color	magickal Properties
		intuition, dreams, femininity, fertility, travel, inspiration, truth
Moss Agate	Green/brown	Abundance, prosperity, wealth, new beginnings, healing, balancing
Obsidian	Black	Protection, spiritual detox, purifying, wards against negativity, eases tension
Rose Quartz	Pink	Self-love, compassion, the heart (physical and spiritual), self-care, healing, tenderness, forgiveness, beauty
Selenite	White	Highly cleansing and purifying—in fact, you can use selenite to cleanse and charge your other crystals
Smoky Quartz	Brown/gray	Grounding, dreams (wards off nightmares), relief from fear and anxiety, healing,

Stone	Color	magickal Properties
		happiness
Tiger's Eye	Yellow/brown	Grounding, protection, luck, abundance, willpower, courage, focus
Turquoise	Blue-green	Calm, communication, articulation, healing, truth, self-realization, guidance

When in doubt, choose a crystal based on its color. If you know you're casting a spell for protection and you've chosen a black candle, chances are, any black crystal you can get your hands on will amplify your intentions of protection.

***

Now, at last, we've covered the practical *and* the magickal, and you're ready for a beginner's book of candle spells.

The best part is that I've prepared you in these past three chapters not just to follow my spell instructions but to truly *understand* where these instructions come from. This empowers you to tweak the spells I've given you to suit your own purposes and the ingredients and materials you have available to you— even to write your own spells from scratch.

The particular elements of candle magick—all these herbs, runes, crystals, and even varieties of flame—may seem like a lot of information to take in at once. And that's okay! You don't need to memorize anything. Witchcraft is intuitive, not intellectual. The best thing you can do to build your skill and knowledge is to practice; over time, correspondences and ritual tools will become second nature to you as they have to me. Stick with the spells I've given you to start, tweak them here and there where you're confident, and branch out into your own spells when you feel ready.

So, let's cast some spells!

Part II: A New Witch's Candle Spellbook

Chapter 4: Candle Spells for Love and Relationships

Come-to-Me Candles

This powerful candle spell will bring a lover to you, harnessing your innate powers of manifestation to draw in all the love (and passion) you deserve. What this spell *won't* do is make any *particular* person love and desire you—that's a dangerous game I don't recommend playing! But if you cast this spell with an open heart and an open mind, I guarantee the Universe will bring romance into your life—perhaps where you least expect it.

- **Timing:** Begin at the waning moon, nine days before the full moon

- **Duration:** Nine days

- **Materials:** 2 taper or pillar candles: one red, one pink; patchouli essential oil; crushed, dried rose petals and jasmine flowers; athame or another tool for carving; if you have a deck of tarot cards, pull the Lovers out and place it on your altar for this spell

Instructions:

1. Cleanse your altar with smoke, holy water, or a ringing bell. Take a cleansing breath and ground and center yourself.

2. Set up your altar so that the two candles are on either side of the Lovers tarot card. If you do not have a tarot deck, you can leave the space between candles empty or place another meaningful object there on which to focus your intention to draw a lover to you.

3. Using your athame or another carving tool, first carve the rune *wunjo* (ᚹ) into the red candle. Anoint the red candle in patchouli and dress it in dried jasmine flowers. The red candle represents the passionate, sensual side of your love.

4. Next, repeat the process for the pink candle, carving the rune *gebo* (X) into it. Anoint the pink candle in patchouli and dress it in dried, crushed rose petals. The pink candle and its trappings represent the intimate caring side of your love.

5. Now, light both candles, beginning with the red. As you do so, say this incantation aloud:

Come to me, come to me,

Passion burning bright.

Come to me, come to me,

Tender love so right.

Come to me, come to me,

Partner in my sights. So mote it be.

6. Finally, let the candles burn and meditate on the kind of relationship you're looking for. Try not to focus on the qualities of your potential partner; instead, conjure in your mind's eye the sensations of being in passionate love.

7. When you feel the meditation is complete, snuff out both candles.

8. Repeat steps 5-7 each evening for nine days, up to and including the evening of the full moon. After the full moon, dispose of any remaining bits of candle that you have not used up. If you choose to repeat the spell during the next moon cycle for added effect, start fresh with new candles.

Honey Jar Attraction Spell

Spell jars are a popular tool in witchcraft, and this one in particular relies on the magick of candles to be cast. A honey jar makes others "sweet" on you—get it? It works by increasing your *own* magnetism, letting your irresistible personality shine out from within, which will naturally attract others to you. This is a safe alternative to a spell meant to attract a specific person to you; you've seen in pop culture how sour a love spell can turn, right? As a bonus, this honey jar works on both romantic interests and friendships, based on what precisely you want to invite into your life.

- **Timing:** Weekly on Fridays

- **Duration:** Time to prepare jar, plus time for the candle to burn down—about two hours

- **Materials:** A piece of paper and pen; 1 pink chime candle; small glass jar with lid; a cup of honey; a small magnet; a pinch of each of these herbs: althea (marshmallow root), balm of Gilead, cinnamon, honeysuckle, and lemon balm

Instructions:

1. Begin by writing your intentions down on the slip of paper. Write your intentions in the present tense, as though you already have what you want, like "I draw in true friends who lift me up and inspire me," or perhaps "I am loved for precisely who I am. My soulmate is drawn to

me." When you're finished, fold the piece of paper three times.

2. Then energetically cleanse your jar as well as your altar with smoke, such as from burning sage.

3. Next, place all of the herbs, the small magnet, and your slip of paper in the jar. Pour the honey over top and screw the lid on tightly.

4. Light the pink spell candle. Hold it sideways over the lid of the jar so that a few drops of wax fall, and then use the wax to cement the candle upright on top of the jar. As you do so, say aloud:

    Sweet as honey, magnetic attraction,
    Draw unto me my satisfaction. So mote it be.

5. Let the candle burn all the way down.

6. Afterward, store the honey jar on your altar or somewhere in your home where it will go undisturbed.

7. Repeat the spell every Friday, burning a fresh pink candle on top of the lid and reciting the incantation. Do this until your wish is fulfilled and the people you desire are drawn to you.

Rekindling Flames Spell

This powerful (yet beginner-friendly) candle spell can help light a bit of fire in your relationship.

- **Timing:** Full moon

- **Duration:** About 20 minutes

- **Materials:** 2 red chime candles; incense (I suggest jasmine or rose); ylang ylang essential oil; crushed dried rose petals; red string or twine; athame or another carving tool; pen and paper

Instructions:

1. Prepare and cleanse your altar; ground and center yourself.

2. Light some of your preferred incense mindfully. Relax in front of your altar; close your eyes and breathe in the scent of the smoke.

3. Once you're ready to continue, call to mind your intention. It could be something like "Our fire will never be extinguished," or even "Ignite the spark." Whatever words represent the reality you intend to manifest, write them down.

4. Then, follow the instructions in Chapter 3 to create a sigil out of your intention.

5. Carve this sigil into the first candle and your lover's name into the other.

6. Anoint both candles with ylang-ylang oil right and roll them both in dried, crushed rose petals.

7. Set the two candles in holders about two inches apart with the candle representing your lover on the left. Carefully tie the candles together with the red string.

8. Light both candles and allow the flames to grow strong.

9. When you are ready, burn the paper on which you drew the sigil in the flames of *both* candles. <u>Do this very carefully, using a pair of tongs or similar.</u>

10. Finally, snuff out both candles *before* the flames reach the string, taking care to leave the two candles connected with the string you tied before.

11. Leave the tied-together, half-melted candles undisturbed on your altar until the new moon, then bury them.

Chapter 5: Candle Spells for Success and Abundance

Seven-day Candle Spell for Seven Times Wealth

Seven-day candle spells are some of the easiest for a first-time caster because the ingredients are so simple: all you need is a seven-day candle. Recall from Chapter 2 that these are tall, skinny glass jars filled with wax, often called prayer candles. They're a powerful manifestation tool because one candle can burn for such a long time, sending your energy out into the universe all the while. So, with this seven-day candle spell for money, you can reap seven times the reward!

Note: Never leave a candle burning unattended. Snuff out your seven-day candle each time you leave the house or fall asleep; relight it when you return. For this reason, your "seven-day" candle may last longer than seven days.

- **Timing:** Begin on the new moon and burn the candle throughout the waxing moon

- **Duration:** As long as it takes the candle to burn away

- **Materials:** 1 seven-day green spell candle

Instructions:

1. Cleanse your altar and ground and center yourself.

2. Spend a moment visualizing an image of yourself in complete prosperity. Imagine that you have all the money you need, but don't presume to tell the Universe how to go about bringing it to you. Just picture the end result— you with much abundance—plainly in your mind's eye. When you feel ready, light the candle and recite the words:

   Money flow as the green grass grows,
   Nary a worry, my cup overflow. So mote it be.

3. Let the candle burn for as long as you can. Remember, you should never leave a candle unattended—so snuff it out when you leave the house and relight it upon your return. Each time you relight the candle, use the same visualization and incantation.

4. Repeat this ritual nightly until the candle has melted away completely or until the full moon, whichever comes first.

Spell to Release a Creative Block

We all feel a little out of sorts sometimes in regard to our creative work and pursuits. When you just aren't catching any inspiring vibes, try this simple candle and crystal spell. It'll help you release the creative dam, getting your ideas flowing once again.

- **Timing:** New or full moon, or on a Sunday

- **Duration:** About two hours, or until the chime candle burns away

- **Materials:** 1 orange chime candle; a small piece of citrine crystal; peppermint oil

Instructions:

1. Ground and center yourself; cleanse your altar space. Arrange the orange candle in a candle holder on your altar next to the citrine.

2. Carve the rune *inguz* (ᛝ) into the side of your orange chime candle.

3. Anoint the candle with peppermint oil in a downward motion from the tip, as if drawing energy down to you.

4. Drop a single drop of peppermint oil onto your piece of citrine.

5. Light the candle, and as you do so, say the words:

   Creative muses, come to me,
   My eyes, my mind awakening. So mote it be.

6. Visualize yourself at the height of your creative energy as you let the candle burn down. After, keep the anointed piece of citrine in your pocket, or on a necklace.

7. You can recharge the spell every two weeks (on the new and full moon) or every week (on Sunday) as needed with a fresh candle.

Golden Candle Spell for Ambition

If you're gunning for a new job or a promotion, beginning a new business venture, or taking on anything in your life that requires you to flex your ambition, look no further than this candle spell to ensure you live up to your potential and nail that interview or sales pitch.

- **Timing:** On a Thursday during the waxing moon phase

- **Duration:** About two hours, or until the chime candle burns away

- **Materials:** 1 gold chime candle; ground clove; ground cinnamon; patchouli essential oil; lemon essential oil; athame, or another carving tool

Instructions:

1. Carve the rune *sowilo* (ᚺ) into the golden candle with your athame or another tool.

2. Anoint the candle with two drops of patchouli and two drops of lemon essential oil, beginning at the tip of the candle and drawing downward toward you. As you anoint the candle, visualize the shimmering gold seeping into the skin of your hands, imparting its luck and brilliance on you.

3. Next, dress the candle in-ground clove and cinnamon for success. As you do so, picture yourself with everything you desire—imagine you've reached your furthest, most brazen goal!

4. When you have the image clear in your mind, take a deep breath, light the candle, and say aloud:

   Golden fire, golden flame,

Light my way in ambition's name. So mote it be.

5. Spend a few moments gazing into the flame of the candle as it burns. Release any self-doubt or negative thoughts you may have about yourself into the flame and visualize these things burning away to nothing, drifting into the air, never to be seen again.

6. Let the candle burn all the way down and repeat the spell as necessary until your ambitions are realized.

Chapter 6: Candle Spells for Protection and Banishment

Home Blessing and Protection Spell

The ideal time to cast this double-whammy protection and blessings spell for home and hearth is when you move into a new living space, but right after a spring cleaning in your existing home will do, too. You can repeat this spell once annually to recharge its protective power.

- **Timing:** Full moon—also a great spell for Imbolc

- **Duration:** Two days

- **Materials:** 2 black chime candles; 2 white chime candles; 4 small jam jars; dried lavender and basil; salt; rice

Instructions:

1. On the first day of the spell, in the daylight, tidy your home and cleanse the entire space energetically with herb smoke. Open the windows, if you can, and let the fresh air in.

2. Next, ready your four jars and fill each one with one of your four ingredients: dried lavender for peace, dried basil for protection, salt for warding evil away from the home, and rice to invite in good fortune. Seal the lids of the jars.

3. Place the jars in the four cardinal directions within your home, such as on four separate window sills on four sides of the house. If you prefer, you can set the jars outside in the yard at the four corners. Arrange the jars thusly: salt in the north, lavender in the east, basil in the south, and rice in the west. Leave the jars there (on the windowsill or outside) overnight so that they soak up the light of the full moon.

4. The next day, gather your four jars to your cleansed altar. Arrange them again according to the four directions.

5. Next, light a black chime candle, and turn it sideways over the lid of your salt jar in the north. Let several drops of fresh wax fall onto the lid; then, place the candle firmly upright in the melted wax so that it's standing on top of the jar. Repeat this process with a white chime candle for lavender in the east, another black candle for rice in the south, and the second white candle for rice in the west.

6. Once all four candles are lit, say this incantation aloud.

> *Bless this home in peace and love.*
> *Cleansed of all we should be rid of.*
> *Protect those who do dwell here.*
> *Keep us close, safe, and dear. So mote it be.*

7. Finally, let the candles burn all the way down. When the last candle has gone out, place the four jars back in the four corners of your home. Alternatively, you can bury the jars in the four corners of your yard.

8. Repeat annually. You can use the same jars next year; just energetically cleanse them and repeat the candle spell with fresh candles.

Traveling Protection Spell

Use this quick candle spell before any trip away from home to ensure a safe journey, whether you're gone overnight or for a longer trip.

- **Timing:** The evening before your journey, when the moon is out

- **Duration:** About two hours, or until the candle burns away

- **Materials:** 1 white chime candle; rosemary essential oil; black pepper; a piece of moonstone (or sub clear quartz)

Instructions:

1. Cleanse your altar space; ground and center yourself.

2. Anoint your white chime candle in rosemary oil and roll it in ground black pepper for protection.

3. Place the candle in its holder next to the piece of moonstone and light the candle. As you do so, say:

   By the light of Mother Moon,
   I'll reach my destination soon.
   My trip will safe and blessed be
   For all concerned, as well as me. So mote it be.

4. Let the candle burn all the way down.

5. When complete, place the moonstone crystal in your car or your traveling bag so that it's with you while you're on the move.

6. Leave any candle remains on your altar until you return from your trip; then, bury them.

Cord Cutting Candle Ritual

As painful as it can be, sometimes the best thing we can do for ourselves is to let go of a person we once loved—whether the relationship has run its course or that person was somehow toxic for us. When a relationship ends, if you find yourself struggling to cut that tether and let go of the past, turn to the witches' favorite cord cutting ritual. This is an old ritual in which the energetic cords that bind you to a former friend or partner are cut (or in this case, burned away), releasing you both to face the future rather than holding each other back. In other words, this cord cutting spell helps you make your *own* closure.

- **Timing:** Waning moon

- **Duration:** About two hours, or until the candles burn away

- **Materials:** A fire-safe dish, such as a cauldron or cast-iron skillet; 1 black chime candle; 1 white chime candle; frankincense oil; twine or string; athame or other carving tool

Instructions:

1. Carve your own name into the white candle and the other person's name into the black candle.

2. Anoint both candles with frankincense essential oil, beginning at the bottom and rubbing the oil upwards to the tip as if away from you—banishing.

3. Braid a length of twine or string into a long braid of three strands. As you create the braid, meditate on this relationship—specifically, think about why it is you need to let go. Don't let anger and pain cloud your feelings. Instead, focus on the fact that you're releasing these bad feelings, making a better future for yourself free from the energetic ties that bind you to a painful past.

4. When your braid is about six inches long, stop braiding. Tie each end of the braid to the center of one of the two candles and set the candles a few inches apart in your cauldron or another fire-safe dish.

5. Light the white candle, then the black. As you do so, say the words:

   Flames release the ties that bind.
   I take with me only what is mine. So mote it be.

6. Let the candles burn. When the flame reaches the braid, the twine will begin to burn, too, until the candles are separated and finally melted to only remnants.

7. Bury the remnants of the candles and any twine in the dirt, far away from your home.

Chapter 7: Candle Spells for Healing and Self-Care

White Light Healing Ritual

This spell can help with any kind of ailment you may be facing. It's not intended to take the place of medicine or your medical provider, but it can be a powerful tool alongside these things for chronic or acute pain, injury, illness, or disease. The healing power of white light is fueled by your *own* internal energies, so the more you can relax and focus your intentions for this ritual, the more you'll benefit from its magick.

- **Timing:** Begin on the full moon or a Monday

- **Duration:** 15-20 minutes

- **Materials:** 9 white tealight candles

Instructions:

1. You will need to set aside a bit of space where you can sit, either on the floor or in a chair, with nine candles around you in a circle. Cleanse this space with smoke/incense. Try putting on some ambient music, as well.

2. Set up the candles around your seat, then sit and take in several deep, calming breaths. When you're ready, light the nine candles beginning in the north and moving clockwise.

3. Once all nine candles are aflame, sit back in your seat, close your eyes, and bring your focus to your breath. Visualize nine balls of white light where the candles encircle you. Picture these balls of light growing larger, emanating warmth, and see them send their light into you. Imagine a similar white light glowing in your chest, at your heart's center, fueled by the nine lights around you. Feel the warmth in your chest and visualize the light spreading out from your heart's center to your entire being, focusing on the part of your body in particular that needs healing. Continue to breathe deeply the entire time.

4. Once you feel the visualization is complete, or after about 15-20 minutes of meditation, open your eyes and snuff out the candles.

5. Repeat this ritual daily until the candles have been spent.

Simple Self-Love Booster

The most important relationship to nourish in your life is the one you have with yourself. This simple self-love booster spell can be practiced quickly and easily anytime you need a little reminder of how much you're worthy of love.

- **Timing:** During the waxing moon, on a Friday

- **Duration:** Time for a bath + time for the candle to burn down

- **Materials:** 1 pink chime candle; honeysuckle essential oil; a small crystal of rose quartz

Instructions:

1. Start by taking a cleansing bath; this is a great way to begin *any* self-love spell. It doesn't have to be anything fancy; run yourself a bath, perhaps with a nice bath bomb or some oils, light a candle if you please. As you soak, release any lingering negative vibes—feel them melt into the water and see them running down the drain afterward. If you're short on time, take a mindful shower, visualizing the hot water washing away all negative energies.

2. After your bath or shower, briefly smoke cleanse your altar. Take a cleansing breath and ground and center yourself.

3. Anoint your pink spell candle with the honeysuckle essential oil, beginning at the tip of the candle and drawing oil downward.

4. Place the candle in its holder and light it.

5. Take your piece of rose quartz in your hand and (very carefully) pass it through the candle's flame three times. As you do so, repeat this incantation:

    I am love, I am loved, I am lover. So mote it be.

6. Next, set the crystal down in front of the candle on your altar. Let the candle burn.

7. When the candle has melted away, take the piece of rose quartz from your altar. You can carry this with you on your person or in your purse—or try sleeping with it under your pillow. If you feel the need for another boost, you can repeat this spell at the next waxing moon.

Candle Spell for Sweet Dreams

This spell does double-duty, warding off nightmares and promoting restful sleep. You can cast this on yourself or on someone else, such as if your child is prone to nightmares. It's quick and easy to cast, so you can even do it right in the moment of need, late at night when awoken from a bad dream. Repeat this spell as often as needed for sweet dreams!

- **Timing:** Before bed, or as needed in the middle of the night

- **Duration:** Just a few minutes

- **Materials:** 1 lavender candle votive, taper, or pillar candle; a length of silver ribbon

Instructions:

1. Cleanse your space before bed—both energetically *and* practically. Make sure you have a comfortable space, such as with clean sheets, cozy pillows, and maybe soothing music or soft lights.

2. Wrap the silver ribbon around your candle and tie it loosely.

3. Light the candle and say aloud:

By this candle, I do sleep,

Nestled snugly, night so deep.

Mother Moon, guide my dreams,

Safe beneath your silver beams. So mote it be.

4. Let the candle burn for just a few minutes. As it burns, visualize yourself (or your loved one) sleeping peacefully. You may even put yourself in your mind's eye within a pleasant dream you remember from the past.

5. Finally, snuff out the candle and unwind the ribbon.

6. Tie the ribbon around your wrist (or your child's wrist) before sleep.

7. Repeat the spell as often as needed for sleep dreams. You can reuse the same materials until your candle is used up.

Farewell

You've made it to the end of the book! I have to thank you sincerely for accompanying me on this journey. Whether you're a seasoned witch looking to up her candle game or a brand-new doe-eyed baby witch picking up a Wicca book for the first time, I hope you've learned a thing or two and walked away with some spells for your grimoire!

If you enjoyed this little book and took something away from it, please take the time to leave a review. Your honest review helps my book reach more witches, so it's a great way for you to pay it forward. And if you're the kind of witch who likes to pay it forward, well, you're my kind of witch, indeed.

Blessed be!

References

Bishop, Bridget. *The Candle Magic Spell Book: A Beginner's Guide to Spells to Improve Your Life (Spell Books for Beginners Book 1)*. Hentopan Publishing, 2020.

Chamberlain, Lisa. *Wicca Book of Candle Spells: A Book of Shadows for Wiccans, Witches, and Other Practitioners of Candle Magic (Wicca Spell Books Series)*. Chamberlain Publications, 2018.

Gaia Staff. "Emerald Tablet 101: The Birth of Alchemy." Gaia.com, March 3, 2020. https://www.gaia.com/article/emerald-tablet-101-the-birth-of-alchemy.

Greenleaf, Ceridwen. "A ritual guide to the days of the week." Ryland Peters & Small, May 16, 2018. https://rylandpeters.com/blogs/health-mind-body-and-spirit/a-ritual-guide-to-the-days-of-the-week

Hicks, Ruth Ilsley. "Egyptian Elements in Greek Mythology." *Transactions and Proceedings of the American Philological Association* 93 (1962): 90–108. https://doi.org/10.2307/283753.

History.com Editors. "Wicca." History.com, August 21, 2018. https://www.history.com/topics/religion/wicca.

Magin Rose. "Exploring the Runes." MaginRose.com. Accessed February 10, 2022. https://www.maginrose.com/runes/exploring-the-runes/.

Wigington, Patti. "The Rule of Three." Learn Religions, February 21, 2018. https://www.learnreligions.com/rule-of-three-2562822.

Wigington, Patti. "The Wiccan Rede." Learn Religions, December 23, 2018. https://www.learnreligions.com/the-wiccan-rede-2562601.

Printed in Great Britain
by Amazon

31382888R00059